Contents

All Channel 4's programmes for schools are subtitled on Teletext for the deaf and hearing-impaired.

Introduction	About **Star Maths**	2
	Who's in the series	4

Handling Data

Programme 31	**Eggs in Space** Solving a problem by collecting, organising, representing and interpreting data in a pictogram.	6
Programme 32	**The Lonely Planetoid** Solving a problem by collecting, organising, representing and interpreting data in a bar chart.	8
Programme 33	**A Perfect Fit** Using known number facts and place value to add mentally.	10
Programme 34	**What's the Difference?** Using known number facts and place value to subtract mentally.	12
Programme 35	**It All Adds Up** Carrying out column addition of two 3-digit numbers.	14
Programme 36	**Power Cut** Carrying out column subtraction of two 3-digit numbers.	16
Programme 37	**Leftovers** Finding remainders after division.	18

Solving Problems

Programme 38	**A Waste of Time** Solving a real-life problem involving reading times from clocks.	20
Programme 39	**The Farewell Party** Solving mathematical problems and puzzles.	22
Programme 40	**The Final Mission** Solving a real-life problem involving planning a route.	24
	Resource Sheet 1 Palindromes and the Seven Times Table	26
	Resource Sheet 2 Time Loop Cards	27
	Resource Sheet 3 Co-ordinate Pictures	28
	Credits	Inside back cover

We are always pleased to receive constructive comments and suggestions about both the series and the support materials.
Please write to **Liz Meenan,** Education Officer, 4Learning, PO Box 444, London SW1P 2WD

STAR MATHS INTRODUCTION

About Star Maths

Underlying ideas and aims

The programmes and resources have been designed to:

- give a focused and stimulating selection of ideas and starting points for maths work in the classroom
- support direct teaching and interactive oral work with the whole class
- provide teachers with a flexible set of resources which can be used alongside any infant maths scheme
- encourage discussion of ways to tackle problems
- emphasise mental calculation
- develop children's understanding and use of mathematical vocabulary
- engage, stimulate and challenge children and encourage them to become more confident in their mathematics work
- suggest cross-curricular links, especially with English and music.

Structure

The Star Maths series is split into two units of ten 10-minute programmes for each of the two year groups in the 7–9 age range. The units reflect the key areas of the National Numeracy Framework and the programmes focus on key objectives. The topics covered for 8–9 year olds in **Star Maths Part 4** (and Part 3) are:

Numbers and the number system

- counting
- properties of numbers and number sequences
- place value and ordering, including reading and writing numbers
- estimating and rounding
- fractions, decimals, their equivalence; ratio and proportion

Calculations

- understanding number operations and relationships
- rapid recall of number facts
- mental calculation, including strategies for deriving new facts from known facts
- pencil and paper methods
- checking that results of calculations are reasonable

Measures, shape and space

- measures, including choosing units, reading scales and time
- properties of 2D and 3D shapes, position, direction and movement

Handling data

- collecting, presenting and interpreting numerical data

Solving problems

- making decisions; deciding which operation and method of calculation to use
- reasoning about numbers and shapes and making general statements about them
- solving problems involving numbers in context: 'real life', money, measures and puzzles

The programme units are based on the National Numeracy Framework (which is based on the Mathematics National Curriculum for England and Wales), but all programmes are equally applicable to the mathematics curricula of England, Wales, Scotland and Northern Ireland. Furthermore, the programmes are designed for flexible use; they are self-contained so that teachers can select a single programme to support the particular concept they are teaching.

Programme format

Each programme concentrates on a single mathematical idea in a pupil-friendly way (see Contents page), and is made up of three elements:

- An episode from a 3D animated soap opera which is set on Junketir – a planetoid slightly smaller than the Earth's moon, owned by Uncle Zak – where two children, Sam and Amber, are staying because their school space bus has broken down. In each episode the children have an adventure that leads to a challenge which can only be solved by mathematics. Along the way they enlist help from Lisa, the space ferry pilot, eccentric Uncle Zak, and a group of robotic helpers, the Wattbots.

- An animated sequence featuring Numberella, a mathematical oracle who lives somewhere else in space – upon whom the children call when they need advice about maths. Using demonstration, words and music, she leads the children and the viewers through the required mathematics.

- One or two songs/rhymes and catchy music about the mathematical focus of the programme. Songs/rhymes can be an infectious form of 'rote learning'. Through them viewers can learn the mathematical facts by heart, or explore the mathematical idea behind the programme.

Using the programmes

To make best use of the series, we recommend that you buy the available video or record each programme yourself. You can then preview the programmes and decide how best they could support your teaching. This allows for a wide range of teaching styles. The video can then be paused at key points and your pupils can discuss what's happening on screen, predict what's going to happen and answer any questions posed. You can also review particular aspects of programmes as many times as you like. Furthermore, the programmes can become part of your bank of resources to support mathematics work.

One way to use the series is to record the programmes and then:

- Preview each programme and decide on the best time to view with the class.
- Before viewing a programme, revise and talk about the ideas behind it.
- View the programme, maybe pausing where appropriate and encouraging discussion.
- Have a whole-class discussion about ideas raised, and then show all or part of the programme again.
- Follow up with related activities.

The mathematics lesson

For those teachers following the National Numeracy Framework, a typical lesson (about 50–60 minutes) will be structured like this:

- Oral and mental calculation work with the whole class.
- Main teaching activity with the whole class, followed by differentiated group/individual activities.

- A plenary session with the whole class to round off the lesson.

The programmes and support materials fit easily into this lesson structure. These resources will help teachers with the demands of the Framework and add variety to their lessons.

- At the beginning of the lesson, before viewing, the teacher could take some of the ideas and suggestions in this Teachers' Guide and use them for preliminary oral and mental work with the whole class (about 10 minutes' work).

- Next, the class could view one whole programme. Afterwards, with the help of the activities in the Teachers' Guide and Activity Book, explore and discuss the concept that the programme illustrates (about 30–40 minutes' work).

- The lesson can be brought to an end with a whole-class discussion so that the pupils can give their opinions on the programme and activities, review the mathematics they have seen, heard and done, and take stock for the next mathematics lesson (about 10 minutes' work).

STAR MATHS
INTRODUCTION

Who's in the series

The **Star Maths** story is as follows:

On a trip to the Billion Bumps star system, the school space bus breaks down. As there will be a long wait for spares, Sam's parents get in touch with his Uncle Zak. Uncle Zak invites Sam and his friend Amber to stay with him on nearby Junketir, and arranges for Lisa to bring them in her transport ship. Junketir is a planetoid slightly smaller than the Earth's moon. It has a breathable atmosphere and a climate that supports different types of vegetation and animal life. Junketir is owned by Uncle Zak, who salvages and recycles the space junk that he finds there.

Uncle Zak, besides recycling space junk, is an inventor. He is kind and wise and delighted that the children have come to stay. He is also somewhat absent-minded and eccentric, and not too bothered with the niceties of conventional parenting. In fact, he sometimes seems more of a child than Sam and Amber.

Amber likes reading and quiet pursuits and prefers to think things out carefully before taking action. She is often unhappy with Sam's impetuous approach and worries about being associated with some of his schemes, becoming quite bossy if she thinks he is doing the wrong thing. She is very practical and has a gift for mending things.

Sam's curiosity sometimes leads him into mischief; his impetuosity stops him looking before he leaps. He gets frustrated by Amber's slow and methodical approach to problems. Although he isn't so good at logical problem solving, he does have flashes of intuition. He likes to think he is brave and daring but tends to panic in a crisis.

As a transport pilot, **Lisa** has to make deliveries to and collections from Junketir. She is very modest about her past, but we suspect that she has probably performed some hair-raising exploits. She tries to see Sam and Amber as often as possible and is, of course, a role model for them.

Botler is a domestic service robot whose hosepipe arm and bumbag equipment container allow him to perform a wide variety of household tasks. Besides having an encyclopaedic knowledge, he is also able to illustrate his answers to the children's questions on his 3D holographic projector. Unfortunately, much to their amusement, he is subject to occasional 'spark attacks' when his sophisticated programming malfunctions.

- **Spoats** are space goats. Like their terrestrial counterparts, they are very greedy and will eat everything. Uncle Zak keeps four of them in the barn to provide milk.
- **Geecees** are galactic chickens. They live in the barn and provide the colony with eggs.
- **Krizwoks** are creatures that are never actually seen but their presence is suggested by sinister noises and unexplained tracks. For Uncle Zak, Lisa and Botler, Krizwoks are a device for ensuring that the children don't stray too far. The Wattbots are terrified at the mere mention of them.

The **Wattbots** are so-called because they resemble light bulbs, aren't very bright, and are Uncle Zak's workforce. When the children arrive there are fourteen of them but their numbers will rise to twenty-four. They came as a job lot and so some have parts missing or are rather battered. Wattbots can't speak but they can squeak. They can also transmit images via the 'snozcams' on their noses.

The animals on Junketir are an interesting mix:

- **Bondals** are gangly flightless birds that can run very fast. They are extremely curious and will approach humans to find out what is going on. They are harmless – although Sam and Amber don't know that at first!
- **Pozzles**, with the characteristics of a dog, a monkey and a mouse, are agile and small creatures. A particular baby pozzle is featured in the programmes. He is very mischievous, torments Botler a lot and often plays a comic role.

Numberella is a mathematical oracle who lives somewhere else in space. The children call upon her when they need advice about maths. Using demonstration and rhyme, she leads the children and the viewers through the required mathematics.

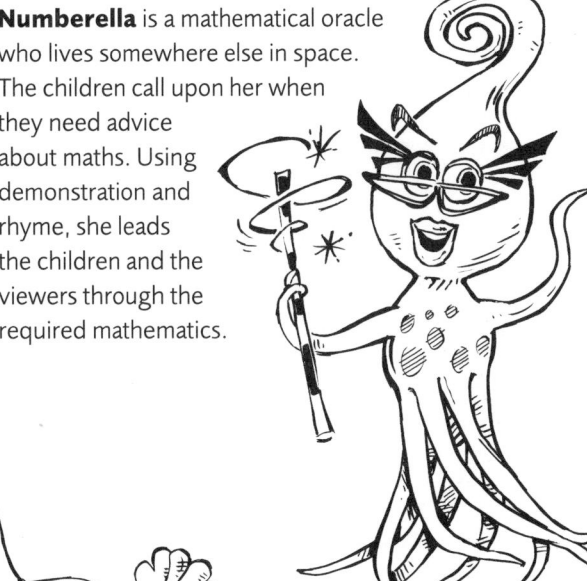

STAR MATHS
PROGRAMME 31

Eggs in Space

Programme outline

Amber and Sam find some 'superfeed' while they are out driving. They decide to feed it to the Geecees to boost their egg production and surprise Uncle Zak. Over the next few days, Sam and Amber get up very early to collect the eggs. They see the egg production increase dramatically.

The children want to show this dramatic rise in egg production to Uncle Zak, without using the actual eggs. With the help of Numberella, Sam and Amber make a pictogram to show the increase in production using an egg symbol to represent five eggs.

Uncle Zak is impressed, both by the pictogram and the increase in productivity. However, he tells the children that superfeed tends to make Geecees rather aggressive. He sends Botler to check whether any of the food is left. Unfortunately, poor Botler receives a rather fierce welcome from these usually docile creatures and leaves the compound in a hurry.

Learning outcomes

Children should gain experience of:

- solving a problem by collecting, organising and representing data in pictograms
- using a symbol to represent several units

Vocabulary

count   pictogram
data   represent
diagram   symbol
key   tally
order   title

Before viewing

☐ Talk to the children about surveys they may have done previously. Make a survey of a topic (for example, how they travel to school). Ask for a show of hands and display the results quickly using a pictogram, with a symbol such as a square or circle to represent two children. Discuss how to show odd numbers of children by using half a square or a semicircle.

While viewing

☐ Pause the video, if you wish, when Sam and Amber are making their pictogram. Amber says that on Thursday there were ten eggs, so she will draw two egg symbols, and on Friday there were 20 eggs. Ask the children how many egg symbols Amber should draw for Friday.

After viewing

Recap

- Talk through the programme with the class. Encourage the children to put what they have seen and heard in their own words. Help them describe what happened by asking questions like:
  - Why were Amber and Sam so keen to make a pictogram?
  - How many days did they have to wait before the superfeed started to work?
  - How many days did Uncle Zak think it would take for the Geecees to get back to normal?
  - The egg production increased in fives so Amber and Sam were able to show complete egg symbols every day. What if they had only three eggs on some days, what could they have done then?

Showing accurate information on pictograms

- Have a whole-class session discussing how information could be displayed using a pictogram but trying to give as accurate a picture as possible. Collect about 100 beads of four or five different colours and put them in a transparent box or plastic bag. Agree with the class that you will use one circle to represent four beads.

- Write the pictogram's title on the board, the key and the different colours down the side.

| Title: colour of beads in bag |
| Key: ◯ represents 4 beads |
| red |
| blue |
| white |
| yellow |
| green |

Ask the class to predict the number of beads in each colour. Then ask several members of the class to come and count them. Enter the correct number of symbols for each colour.

- Extend the work by linking the need for accurate information to the use of different symbols that might be appropriate. For example, use a quarter of a circle to show one bead, a semicircle for two beads and three-quarters of a circle for three beads.

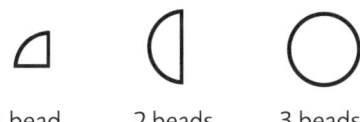

1 bead   2 beads   3 beads

- Spend some time asking the children to interpret the information shown on the pictogram. Ask questions such as:
  - What colour were most beads?
  - How many more red ones than green ones?
  - How many beads were there altogether?

- Follow up the whole-class work with individual or paired work on a variety of topics interesting to the children. Pictograms can be presented in a horizontal or vertical format, and using interesting symbols can make the presentation of information attractive – an important factor in today's 'advertising industry'.

- Ideas for pictograms could include representing birds that visit the bird table, how the children come to school, and how many of them have roller blades or scooters. Suggest bird or car outlines, faces or stick figures to represent people, fruit or vegetable shapes for surveys of food and so on. Help the children design a tally sheet and think about appropriate numbers to use in their survey to represent the data. Encourage some of the children to make a large-scale version of their pictogram, which could be displayed in the classroom. Other children then discuss information that can be gained from the pictogram.

Venn or Carroll diagrams

- Children could be asked to transfer information they used to make a pictogram into a Venn or Carroll diagram. Discuss with them which diagram shows the information better.

More activities

- See the Star Maths 4 Activity Book for other games and activities.

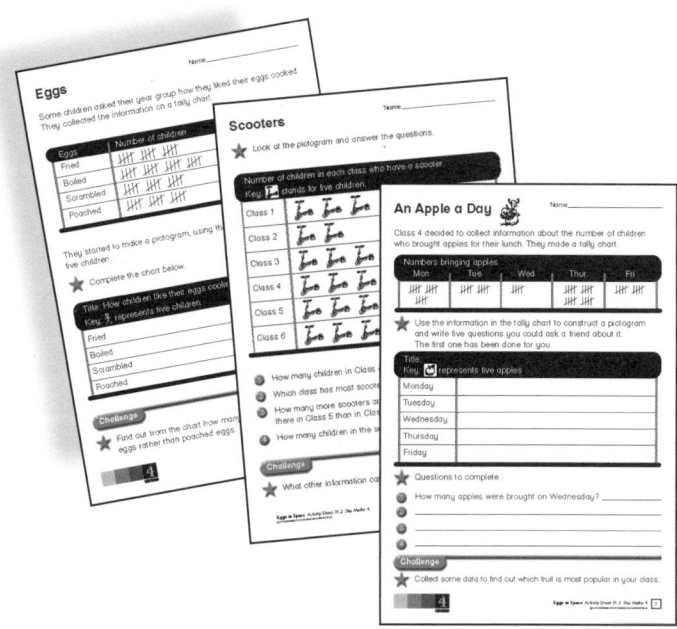

STAR MATHS PROGRAMME 32

The Lonely Planetoid

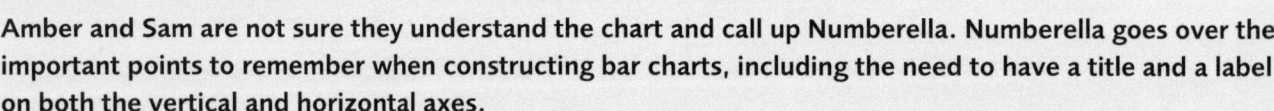

Programme outline

Botler is very disheartened when he sees the information sent to Junketir by the Inter-Galactic Tourist Board. From the bar chart they sent, it is apparent that other planetoids have many more visitors than Junketir. Botler is horrified to see Junketir had only five visitors and wants to attract more.

He sets about making a video, describing the advantages of Junketir as a tourist spot, much to the dismay of Uncle Zak who does not want more visitors. Botler sees the advantage of using a bar chart to convey information about the planetoid and produces one to show the amount of junk falling during each of the three seasons (Misty, Stormy and Sunny).

Amber and Sam are not sure they understand the chart and call up Numberella. Numberella goes over the important points to remember when constructing bar charts, including the need to have a title and a label on both the vertical and horizontal axes.

Uncle Zak thinks Botler's video will keep tourists away, but he is most upset when he receives another call from the tourist board.

Learning outcomes

Children should gain experience of:

- solving a problem by organising, representing and interpreting data in a bar chart
- using a bar chart with a vertical axis marked in multiples of five

Vocabulary

axes	graph	represent
chart	label	sort
count	list	table
data	most common	tally
diagram	most popular	title

Before viewing

☐ Remind the children of previous work on reading and making bar charts. Make bar charts on the board or OHT using information quickly obtained (for example, the children's attendance in class each day the previous week). Use a vertical axis labelled in twos and ask relevant questions like:

- How many children were in class on Monday? Wednesday? Thursday?
- Which day had all the children present?
- Which day had most absences?
- Was there any particular reason for this?
- Was the same pattern being followed this week?

While viewing

☐ Pause the video, if you wish, when Numberella wishes Sam and Amber good luck and says they should be able to interpret the bar chart Botler has prepared. Ask if anyone in the class would like to attempt an interpretation of any information contained in Botler's chart.

After viewing

Recap

- Encourage the children to describe in their own words what they have seen and heard. Ask questions like:
  - Why was Botler keen to make a video of Junketir?
  - What information in the tourist board bar chart made him particularly angry?
  - What had he included in the video?
  - Why did he want to include a bar chart?
  - Why did Uncle Zak mind?
  - Who can remember what advice Numberella gave Amber and Sam about bar charts?

- Make a copy of the bar charts from the tourist board and the one made by Botler on the board or OHT. Ask the children to look at them closely and tell you what information they can get from them, as well as describing the important points about making bar charts.

Reading and interpreting data

- Continue the holiday theme and ask the children to collect holiday brochures and look for lists of hours of sunshine, monthly average temperatures and rainfall. Why are these pieces of information important when deciding where to take a holiday?

- Make a display of the information collected, perhaps adding more information gained from the Internet. Show one of the bar charts to the whole class and ask if anyone can 'tell a story' from the chart. Ask the children to look at it for a few minutes, then talk about it with a neighbour. Afterwards, go round the class and ask some questions. Children find it is easier to compare quantities if they are side by side. They find it more difficult to compare bars that are further apart. Remind children of the scale used on the vertical axis.

Constructing bar charts

- Ideally, children should construct bar charts when they have some information they wish to display clearly. By the age of seven or eight, children are expected to be able to read graphs that have different scales. They should be able to solve a problem by interpreting a bar chart with a vertical axis marked in multiples of 2, 5, 10 or 20.

- Collecting information about themselves and classmates makes data handling relevant and interesting. Sometimes too much emphasis is put on the construction of the graphs and not enough on interpreting the data. Both aspects are important. Start the work by encouraging the children to test a hypothesis such as:

  'more children come to school by bus than by car'.

- Discuss what information would be needed before a decision could be made and help the children to design a questionnaire to find the information they need. Decide on the number of children to be asked and the scale to be used to present the data. If all the children in the school are to be included, then the children need to discuss what scale would be most appropriate.

- Other subjects that appeal to children would be favourite foods, drinks, pets, toys, computer games and so on. Some science projects could help to make important cross-curricular links. These projects could include making weekly measurements of pets or plants and making a bar chart of observations at the end of a term or half term.

- Encourage the children to use computer software to organise and display information they have collected, as well as encouraging them to interpret the information displayed.

More activities

- See the Star Maths 4 Activity Book for other games and activities.

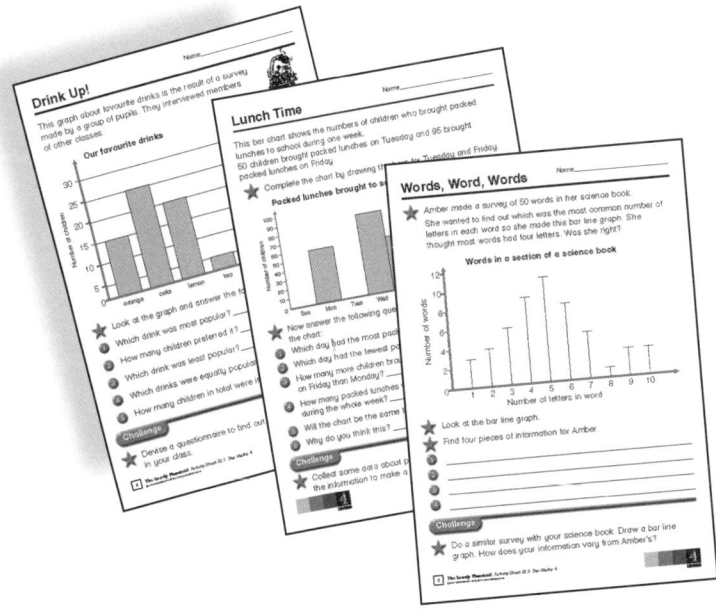

STAR MATHS
PROGRAMME 33

A Perfect Fit

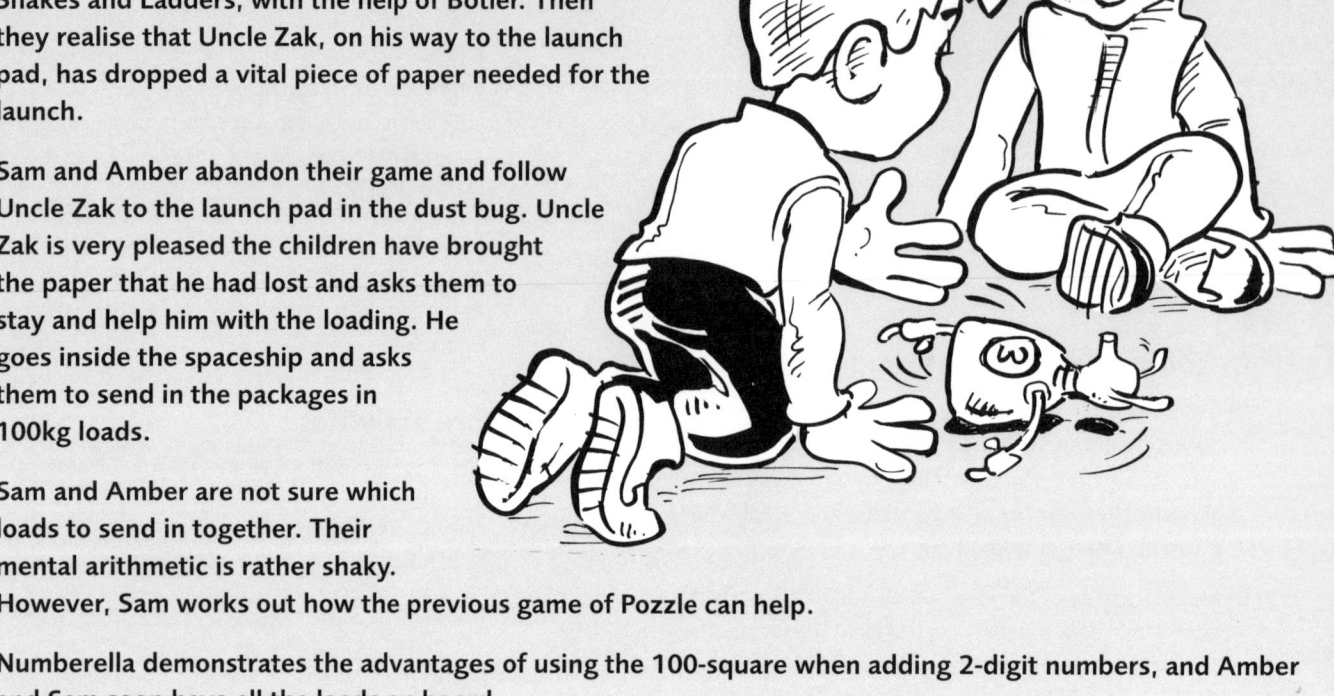

Programme outline

Amber and Sam are playing Pozzle, a space version of Snakes and Ladders, with the help of Botler. Then they realise that Uncle Zak, on his way to the launch pad, has dropped a vital piece of paper needed for the launch.

Sam and Amber abandon their game and follow Uncle Zak to the launch pad in the dust bug. Uncle Zak is very pleased the children have brought the paper that he had lost and asks them to stay and help him with the loading. He goes inside the spaceship and asks them to send in the packages in 100kg loads.

Sam and Amber are not sure which loads to send in together. Their mental arithmetic is rather shaky. However, Sam works out how the previous game of Pozzle can help.

Numberella demonstrates the advantages of using the 100-square when adding 2-digit numbers, and Amber and Sam soon have all the loads on board.

Learning outcomes

Children should gain experience of:

- the mental addition of 2-digit numbers
- the importance of place value
- using known facts to add mentally

Vocabulary

altogether
how many more to make?
sum
total

Before viewing

☐ Spend some time with the children rehearsing previous experience in adding mentally. Encourage the children to have a mental picture of a number and the number ten more or ten less than that number. Ask questions like:

- Which number is ten more than 42?
- Ten less than 67?
- Give me two numbers that have a difference of 10.
- Start counting at 53 and count forwards in tens.
- Start counting at 97 and count back in tens.

While viewing

☐ Stop the video, if you wish, when Numberella says that Sam worked out how to make any number up to 100 by looking at a 100-grid. Ask if anyone in the class would like to demonstrate how this works.

After viewing

Recap
☐ Spend time going over the action of the programme. Encourage the children to put in their own words what they have seen and heard. Ask questions like:
- Why was Sam getting impatient with Amber while they were playing Pozzle?
- Why did they break off the game and join Uncle Zak at the launch pad?
- Explain how Sam found the Pozzle game useful when Uncle Zak wanted the packages sent into the ship in pairs that added to 100kg.
- How did Numberella demonstrate using a 100-square to add any pair of 2-digit numbers?

Numberella
☐ Have a session repeating the action demonstrated by Numberella when adding two 2-digit numbers using a 100-square. Children can follow up the whole-class session with work in pairs, using small number grids.

Throwing numbers
☐ Have a whole-class session working mentally on two numbers that together add to 100. These are called complements of 100. You start by 'throwing' or calling out a 2-digit number (start with a multiple of ten) and the class, in unison, have to 'throw' back the number that makes it up to 100. Move from multiples of ten to multiples of five, then numbers near to a multiple of ten, eg 29 or 31. Keep the action lively and keep going until the numbers become too difficult for most of the class to keep up.

☐ A variation on this theme is to give pupils a set of place value cards and have them 'show' the number that makes your number up to 100.

Display a large 100-square
☐ Extend the work from complements of 100 to adding any pair of 2-digit numbers. Again, start with some easy examples, such as adding a multiple of ten, or a near multiple of ten, before moving on to more difficult numbers.

Problem solving
☐ Children need to be able to use and apply these skills in a variety of contexts in mathematics and other subjects. Divide the class into several teams. Put up some 2-digit plus 2-digit additions on the board and ask each team to make up some problems for the addition by using money, measures of length or weight. Each team concentrates on one particular measure. After allowing some time for the children to think of appropriate contexts, bring the whole class together and ask each group to read out some of their problems.

Right or wrong?
☐ Write up several addition statements on the board or OHT. Include several statements that have wrong answers. Children work in pairs to check which statements are correct and which are wrong. After most of the class have completed the task, go round and discuss the answers. Ask the children to explain how they checked the statements and how they knew which statements were wrong.

More activities
☐ See the Star Maths 4 Activity Book for other games and activities.

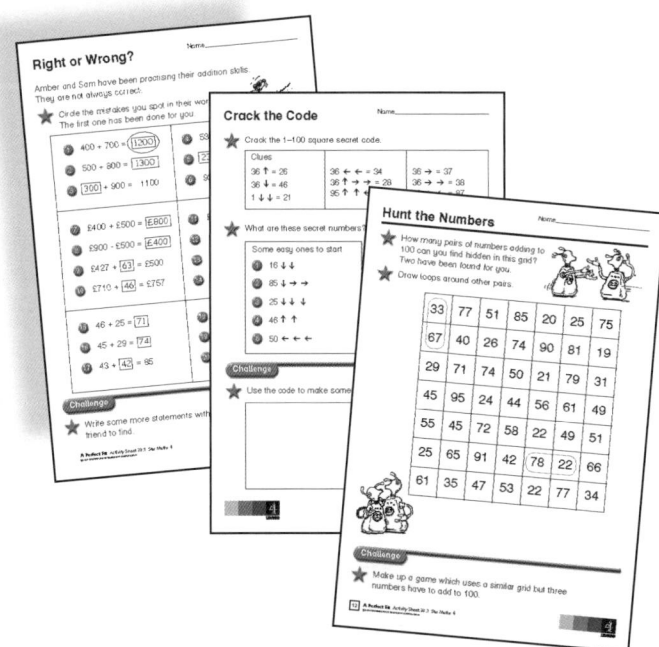

STAR MATHS
PROGRAMME 34

What's the Difference?

Programme outline

Sam and Amber are out on the junk plain collecting junk with some Wattbots. Sam asks one of the Wattbots to throw some junk away and this gives him a brilliant idea – the Junk Throwing Olympics. Sam and Amber each have a team of Wattbots. The idea is to get the Wattbots to throw a piece of junk as far as possible. Amber's team wins the first round and Sam's team wins the second round, but they cannot decide who is winning overall, so they call Numberella to settle the dispute.

Numberella explains they need to work out the difference between the two scores and a 100-square is a useful thing to have when working out differences. She shows them how to find a difference by counting on from the lower number.

The competition resumes and one of Sam's Wattbots throws a piece of junk straight towards Uncle Zak's dust truck. Sam is scared. He thinks his uncle will be cross. However, Uncle Zak thinks having the Wattbots throw junk is an efficient way to collect it. Meanwhile, Amber seems to have won the competition.

Learning outcomes

Children should gain experience of:

- subtracting 2-digit numbers by counting on from the lower number
- using known number facts

Vocabulary

decrease
difference between
how many left?
inverse

leave
minus
subtract
take away

Before viewing

☐ Spend some time with the whole class revising mental skills and linking subtraction with the inverse operation, addition. Ask questions like:

- What is the difference between 12 and 24? 30 less than 94?
- Give me a pair of numbers with a difference of 40. Give me another. And another.
- Subtract 45 from 95.

Ask the children to describe how they work out the answers.

While viewing

☐ Pause the video, if you wish, when Amber and Sam decide to call Numberella to decide who is winning the competition. Ask if anyone in the class can work out the relative positions of the two teams.

After viewing

Recap

- Talk through the programme with the children. Encourage them to use their own words to describe what they have seen and heard. Help them by asking questions like:
  - How did Sam get his idea for the Junk Throwing Olympics?
  - How successful was his strategy with the Wattbots?
  - Why were Sam and Amber unsure who was winning after two rounds?
  - What strategy did Numberella suggest for working out differences?

Using 100-squares and number lines

- Talk about Numberella's idea for using the 100-square. Follow up whole-class work with individual or paired work, using desktop squares.
- Alternatively, some children may prefer to use a numbered or unnumbered number line rather than a 100-square.

Subtraction stories

- Have a class book of subtraction 'stories'. These can be collected over the term as the children develop their subtraction skills. Situations can range from those involving passengers getting on and off a bus, to working out how much money is left after paying for a meal or several items from a shop or mail order catalogue. If there is time, ask the children to illustrate some of their stories.

Using a target board

- Display a collection of numbers on a flipchart, an OHT or the board. Then give the class a task – they have to subtract 30, 35 or 37 from each of the numbers and write down the answers as quickly as they can. Divide the class into groups and adjust the difficulty of the task to suit different abilities. Extend the activity by using 3-digit numbers.

Subtraction bingo

- Write about 25 2-digit numbers, above 20, on the board or flipchart. The children each have a piece of paper and choose 16 of the numbers to make a bingo card.

Tell the children you are going to call out some numbers and they have to subtract 20 from them. Call out at random any of the numbers on the board adding 20 each time. If the children have the number on their card they cross it out. The first to cross out all the numbers is the winner. Play the game again and extend it by adding 19 or 21 to each of the numbers.

Riddles

- Have a collection of 'number riddles' for the children to do. Include questions like:

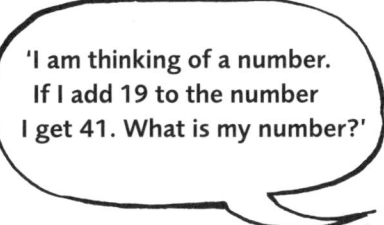

'I am thinking of a number. If I add 19 to the number I get 41. What is my number?'

Ask the children to make up some number riddles for their friends to do.

'The difference is nineteen'

- Have the children working in pairs or small groups to work on possible answers to the statement. What could the two numbers be? You may wish to leave this activity as open-ended as this or restrict the numbers to 2-digit numbers. Display the children's work on a large poster.

More activities

- See the Star Maths 4 Activity Book for other games and activities.

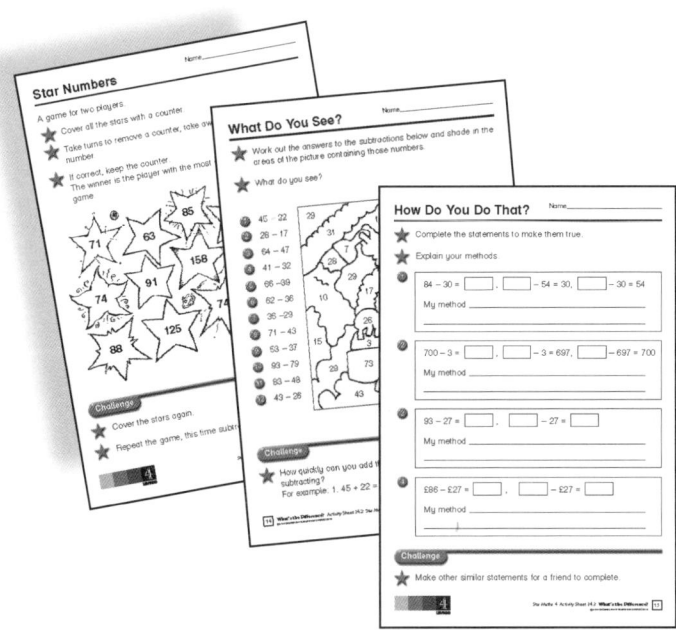

STAR MATHS
PROGRAMME 35

It All Adds Up

Programme outline

Amber and Sam are in the workshop and find an old adding machine that doesn't work. They mend it, but when they show Lisa what it can do, they realise it is not working properly. Uncle Zak arrives rather hurriedly. He is wearing his beekeeper outfit and is very pleased to present them with a small jar of Junketir jam, a kind of honey. Sam tastes it and declares it delicious.

The children and Lisa have similar beekeeper outfits to wear when Uncle Zak takes them to see where this delicious jam comes from. Successful production depends on each hive having between 850 and 900 Prebbies. Uncle Zak, anxious to discuss marketing strategy with Lisa, leaves Sam and Amber to fill some jars from the hives.

Unfortunately Amber, startled by a buzzing Prebbie, knocks over the hives. The resulting chaos has Prebbies buzzing everywhere. Sam and Amber use the Wattbots to return the Prebbies to the hives, but cannot check the numbers quickly enough. They call Numberella for help.

Numberella demonstrates how to add two 3-digit numbers together by keeping one number just as it is and splitting the other number into hundreds, tens and units. Fortunately, Amber and Sam manage to return the correct number of Prebbies back to the hives before Uncle Zak reappears with the old adding machine – now working correctly.

Learning outcomes

Children should gain experience of:

- adding two 3-digit numbers, starting from the most significant digits

Vocabulary

3-digit numbers   altogether
add   sum
addition   total

Before viewing

- ☐ Spend some time talking about 2- and 3-digit numbers. Check what experience the children have of adding numbers mentally. Ask questions like:

- What number do you get when you add 80 and 2? Add 40 to 53.

- What number must I add to 82 to make 102?
- What number must I add to 47 to make 89?
- What is 300 plus 22?
- What is 500 plus 81?

Ask the children to explain how they worked out their answers.

While viewing

- ☐ Pause the video, if you wish, when Sam and Amber call Numberella. Ask if anyone in the class can help them with the problem.

After viewing

Recap

☐ Give the children time to reflect on what they have seen and heard. Encourage them to put in their own words what happened to Amber and Sam and how they solved the problem of the Prebbies. Ask questions like:

- Why was Uncle Zak so pleased when he brought some Junketir jam for Amber and Sam to taste?
- How many Prebbies had to be in each hive to ensure maximum production?
- Why did Sam and Amber have to call Numberella?
- What advice did Numberella give?

☐ Have a whole-class session adding numbers using Numberella's method. Use numbers the children can add mentally before moving on to numbers that involve carrying.

Target board

☐ Have a grid of 3-digit numbers on the board.

400	671	300	804	542
291	100	491	565	800
376	892	211	600	735
120	700	905	475	222

Divide the class into two teams of equal ability. The task is to add numbers like 200 or 210 to the numbers in the first place, then move on to adding more difficult numbers. You call out one of the numbers and ask one of the team members to add 200 or 210. Teams get a point for each correct answer. Adjust the level of questioning to the ability of the team member and increase the difficulty as appropriate.

☐ After an oral session with the whole class, ask the children to work in pairs adding a 3-digit number, such as 235, to all of the numbers. They can use paper and a pencil if they wish. After allowing time for most of the class to complete the task, call the class together and ask for answers. Discuss the different ways of working.

Playing cards

☐ When pupils are more confident adding two 3-digit numbers, a useful whole-class activity can be generated using a pack of playing cards, with the face cards and the tens cards removed. The aim is for the children to write down two 3-digit numbers that, when added together, become the biggest number possible below 1000.

Ask the children to draw a 3-column grid to show hundreds, tens and units. The cards are shuffled and placed face down. Turn over the top card. The children have to record this digit before the next card is turned over. Play proceeds until six cards have been turned over. Players add their two 3-digit numbers. The winner is the player with the biggest number below 1000.

Variations: The game can be played in groups or pairs. Rules can be changed to find the lowest possible number or a specific number, say the number nearest to 700. Dice or 0–9 digit cards can be used to generate the numbers instead of playing cards.

Palindromes

☐ Introduce palindromic numbers such as 767 or 434. Show the class how to make palindromic numbers.

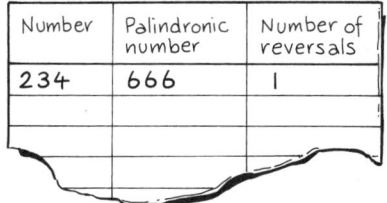

Write a 3-digit number (eg 234)　　234
Reverse the digits 432　　　　　　+ 432
Add the two numbers together　　 666

Some numbers do not become palindromes immediately. Repeat the process until the number eventually becomes palindromic.

☐ You could start a whole-class investigation into 3-digit numbers and how many reversals are needed to make them palindromic. The children's work, when it has been checked by a partner, could be displayed on a chart with these headings:

Number	Palindromic number	Number of reversals
234	666	1

☐ As an extension for your more able pupils, use Resource Sheet 1 on page 26 to explore the link between palindromes and the seven times table.

Decimal numbers

☐ Extend the work to include decimal numbers by giving the children some money problems involving addition. One good activity is to put up a list of prices in a toy shop, burger bar or café and ask the children to work out the cost of several items.

More activities

☐ See the Star Maths 4 Activity Book for other games and activities.

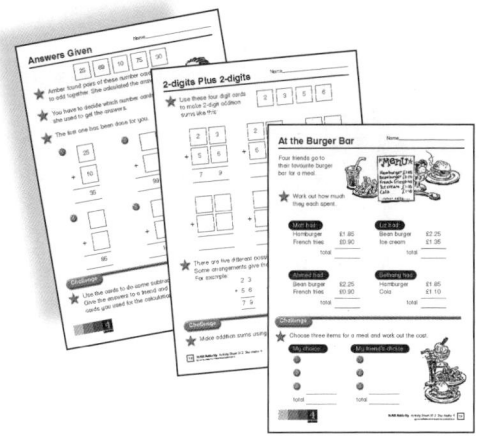

STAR MATHS
PROGRAMME 36

Power Cut

Programme outline

One evening, as Sam and Amber are relaxing, the lights suddenly go out. They hear approaching footsteps in the dark, but it is only Uncle Zak who has come to ask their help to fix a power cut – the cause of the blackout.

Amber and Sam go into an underground passage where the power cable runs. They discover that part of the cable has been eaten away by Weebs, large mouse-like creatures that are not dangerous, but can do a lot of damage to property.

Uncle Zak needs to know exactly how much cable has been damaged, as there are only 352m left in store. The children walk along the cable and see the damage to the cable starts at the 323m mark and continues until the 637m mark. Sam and Amber estimate that about 300m of new cable will be needed, but they have to call Numberella to help them work out the precise amount. Numberella shows them how to work out the difference between the two numbers by adding on. She demonstrates how to use a number line to add on efficiently.

Power is restored, but later in the evening the lights go out again. Sam and Amber decide to go to bed, much to the relief of Uncle Zak and Botler who want a bit of peace and quiet.

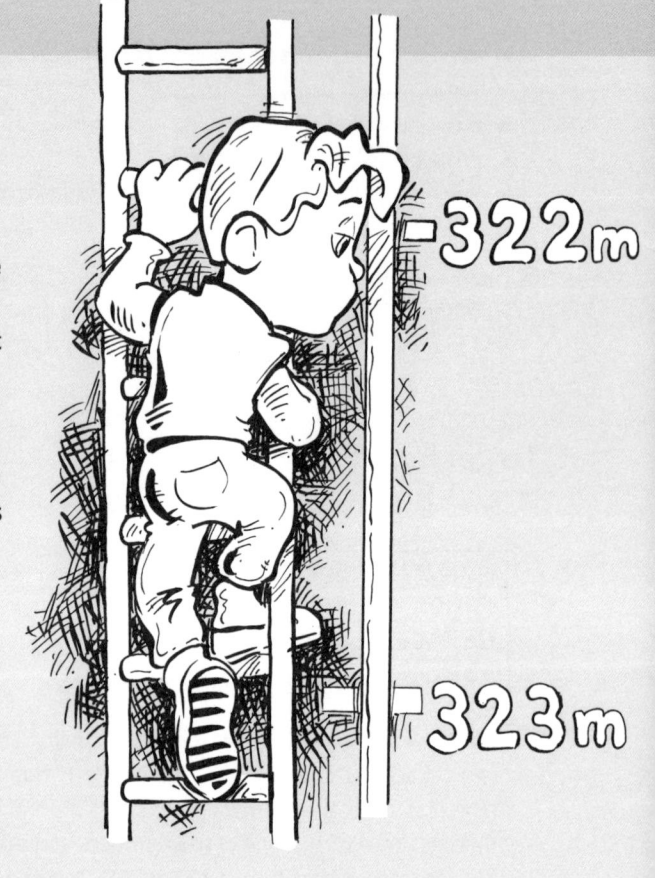

Learning outcomes

Children should gain experience of:

- developing and refining methods of subtraction involving 3-digit numbers

Vocabulary

add
addition
decrease
difference between
inverse

leave
minus
subtract
take away

For example, 83 – 54   29

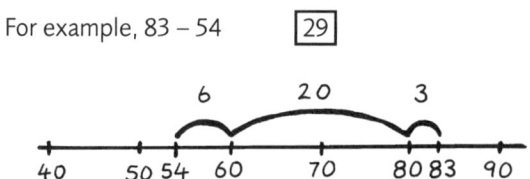

☐ Ask questions like:

- What number must be added to 130 to make 200?
- What must I add to 450 to make 500?

☐ Ask the children to explain how they worked out the answers.

Before viewing

☐ Talk to the children about the different ways of coping with subtraction problems. Spend some time revising methods of subtraction using a number line.

While viewing

☐ Pause the tape, if you wish, when Sam says they need about 300m of cable but Amber reminds him that they need to know exactly how much. Sam knows what to do – he has to subtract 323 from 637 – but doesn't know how and calls Numberella. Ask if anyone in the class could suggest a way of working out the answer to the problem.

After viewing

Recap
☐ Talk through the action with the class. Allow time for the children to reflect on what they have seen and heard. Help them by asking questions like:

- Why did Amber and Sam have to go into the underground passage?
- Why was it important for Uncle Zak to know exactly the length of cable that had been chewed away?
- Why did Amber and Sam call Numberella?
- What did Numberella advise?
- Was there enough cable in the stores to do the repair?
- How much cable was there to spare after the repair? (352m – 314m = 38m)
- How did you work that out?

Number line
☐ Have an unmarked number line on the board and go over the subtractions in the programme.
Introduce other numbers, and after working as a whole class for a time, allow the children to work in pairs or individually on similar calculations.

Spider web subtraction

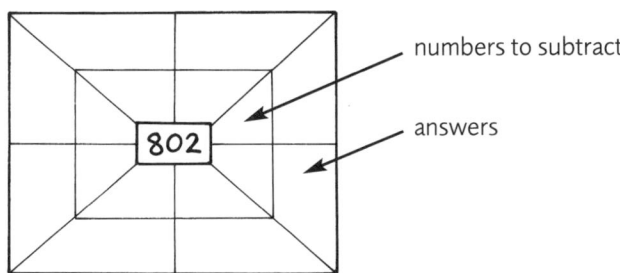

☐ Draw a small rectangle containing a 3-digit number on the board. Surround it with two larger rectangles, as in the diagram. Enter eight smaller 3-digit numbers in the spaces in the second rectangle. Tell the children you want them to subtract the numbers in the second rectangle from the number in the centre.
After allowing some time for the children to work out the answers, go round the class and ask individuals or pairs to come to the board and write the answers in the outer rectangle. Discuss methods of working.

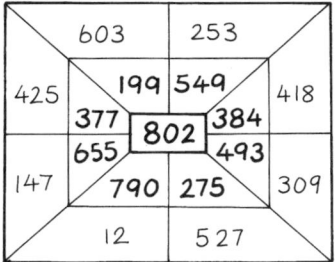

Trace the mistakes
☐ Write some 3-digit subtractions on the board or flipchart. Instead of asking the children to work out the answers, write them in but make several errors. Tell the children you want them to check the subtractions and find the errors. Talk about checking calculations and using the inverse operation.

Money
☐ Money and spending provide many opportunities for oral and paper and pencil work on subtraction. Give the children a fictional amount of money to spend on desirable objects/food in a mail order catalogue or in a burger bar. Ask them to work out how much money they would have left after buying different objects or having certain things to eat.

Story problems
☐ Ask the children to make up some story problems that involve subtraction and 3-digit numbers. The numbers can be decimal numbers if they wish. Make sure they understand that their stories have to be in a meaningful context and they have to know the answers before asking anyone else to work them out. Problems could be written out on small cards or slips of paper and put into a hat. The hat is passed round and pairs of children take out two slips and work out the answers.

More activities
☐ See the Star Maths 4 Activity Book for other games and activities.

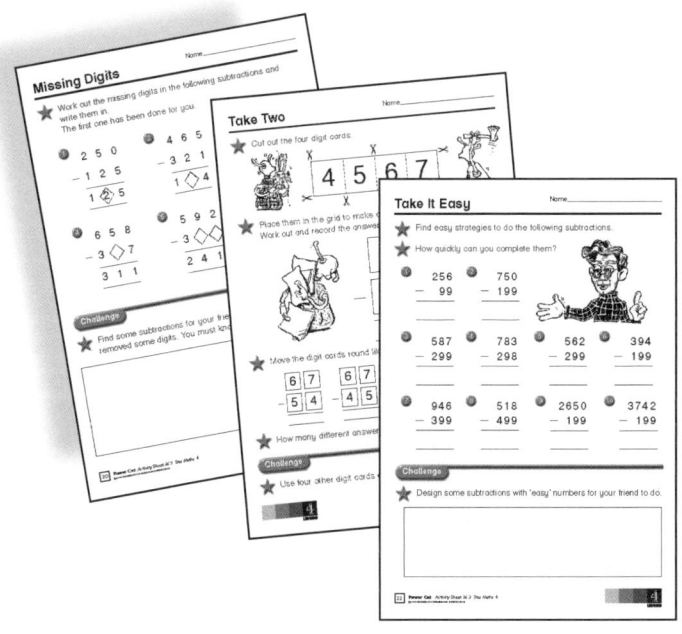

STAR MATHS
PROGRAMME 37

Leftovers

Programme outline

Sam and Amber are playing Robot Rescue, a computer simulation game involving rescuing Wattbots from a danger zone. The two children argue about appropriate strategies and call Numberella.

Numberella explains how Amber, having made the last rescue, should have rounded up the answer to send in four ships so all the Wattbots could be rescued. Numberella reminds Sam and Amber that when they are doing division problems and get a remainder, they must look back at the original question and check that the answer makes sense.

The children and Lisa want to give Uncle Zak a surprise for his birthday, but do not know how to bring in the parcels without his knowledge. Amber persuades Lisa to use a similar strategy to the one Numberella suggested. Uncle Zak is delighted and surprised by his birthday treat.

Learning outcomes

Children should gain experience of:

- problems involving division
- interpreting remainders after division

Vocabulary

array	groups
divide	left over
divided by	lots of
divided into	remainder
divisible by	share
equal groups of	share equally

Before viewing

☐ Revise previous work on division. Link these situations with multiplication, as it is the inverse of division. Give the children a few simple division problems that they can do mentally, such as:

- How many biscuits will I have left after sharing 13 between four children?
- How many lengths of 10cm can I cut from 72cm of ribbon? How much will be left over?
- How many sweets will each child get after sharing 45 between ten?

While viewing

☐ Pause the tape, if you wish, when Numberella, explaining how to cope with division problems that have a remainder, asks what went wrong on Amber's turn. Ask if anyone in the class would like to have a go at explaining what went wrong, before returning to Numberella's explanation.

After viewing

Recap

☐ Spend some time with the class talking about the action. Encourage the children to reflect on what happened by asking questions like:

- Why were Sam and Amber disappointed with their performance on the computer game?
- What mistake had Amber made on the last shot?
- How did Numberella explain what they should have done?
- How did Lisa manage to get Uncle Zak's presents to the base without spoiling the surprise?

Children arrays

☐ Have arrays of children at the front of the class to illustrate various division problems. For example, ask 20 children to come to the front and stand in lines of three, then four, then five, then six, continuing until seven and eight if you think it appropriate. Talk about how many children there are in each row and about the remainder, if there is one.

Discussion of problems

☐ Spend some time as a whole class talking about division problems and whether to round the remainders up or down. Then read out a story sum involving division and rounding. For example:

> 17 children are coming to Lisa's party. Lisa's mum is buying fruit drinks in packs of three. How many packs will she have to buy?

> Farmer Brown has 20 eggs from his hens on Tuesday. He puts six eggs in each box. How many boxes can he fill?

☐ Ask the children to talk to their neighbour about the answer and whether they would round up or round down. Go round the class and collect answers from several pairs before saying which answer is correct.

What number could it be?

☐ Spend some time playing a game with the class where you give them an example of the numbers and clues you want them to use. Put the children into teams to think of questions to ask each other to score points. Suggest questions like:

- I am thinking of a number less than 20 that when divided by five leaves a remainder of two. What number could it be?
- I am thinking of a number between 30 and 50 that when divided by ten has a remainder of five. What number could it be?

Writing 'remainder' problems

☐ Follow up the whole-class work by asking the children to work in pairs to make up some story sums. Ask each pair to write out two problems on slips of paper that are then collected in a bag or hat. The bag is passed round and each pair takes out two problems and works out the answers. After allowing a suitable time for working, go round the class and ask several pairs to talk about their problems, how they solved them and whether they agree with the pair who wrote the original problem.

Remainder challenge

☐ Give the class a challenge to work on, such as:

> Keiran had between 30 and 50 marbles. When he counted them in fours there were two left over. When he counted them in fives there was one left over.
> How many marbles did he have?

Help the children to tackle the problem by linking it to their knowledge of number facts and tables. Go through the multiples of four and add two to each number. List all the multiples of five and add one to each number. Then look for a number that is found in both groups.

More activities

☐ See the Star Maths 4 Activity Book for other games and activities.

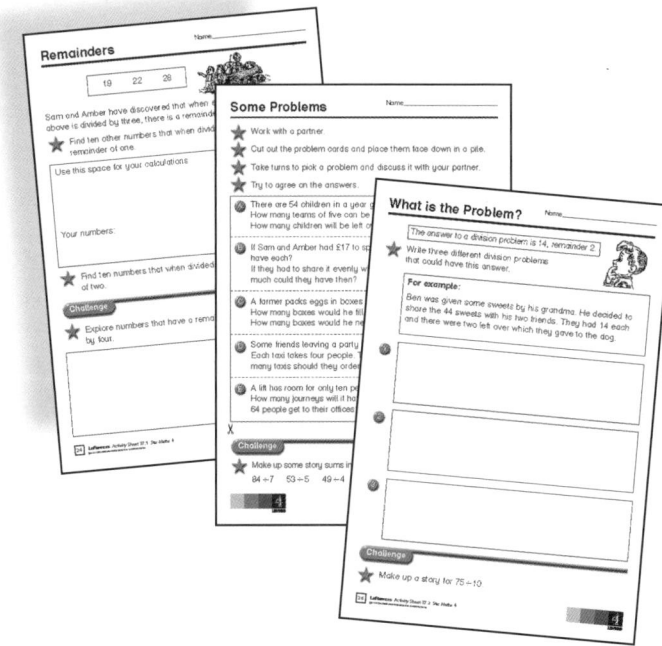

STAR MATHS
PROGRAMME 38

A Waste of Time

Programme outline

A mischievous Pozzle teases Sam and Amber by running off with their clock. As they chase him to get it back, they fall down a large chute in the old recycling system. They cry for help but no one is about to hear them.

They look round and notice a button on the wall. Sam presses it. There is a loud announcement that the junk chute doors will be opened at 10:40am. They call Numberella to explain what it means and how long they may have to wait. The doors open soon after Numberella has disappeared and the two children have yet another fall.

They see a sign about the doors opening but are not sure whether it means in about one hour's time or over twelve hours' time. They pass some time remembering happy incidents on the planetoid until Amber realises she is very hungry and the doors have not opened, so it could mean a long wait before her next meal.

Amber notices a panel on the wall with a control box displaying the time 23:55. The children call Numberella who explains about the 24-hour clock. With Sam supporting her, Amber manages to change the figures on the control mechanism and they suddenly find themselves free, but dumped, unceremoniously, in a heap at the feet of Uncle Zak and Botler.

Learning outcomes

Children should gain experience of:

- solving real-life problems involving time
- reading time from digital and analogue clocks
- am and pm when using analogue clocks

Vocabulary

am
analogue
clock
digital
half past
hands
hour
how long will it be to...?
minute
o'clock
pm
quarter past
quarter to
second
timer
watch

Before viewing

☐ Talk to the children about telling the time using digital and analogue watches and clocks. Have a clock face to display different times. Ask questions like:

- How many days in a week?
- How many hours in a day?
- How many minutes in an hour?
- How many seconds in a minute?
- What can you do in one minute? In five minutes?
- How long do you spend in school in the morning?

☐ Use the time loop cards on Resource Sheet 2 (page 27) to practise simple time problems involving adding and subtracting times.

While viewing

☐ Pause the tape, if you wish, when Amber and Sam have discovered the control panel that displays 23:55 and they call Numberella for the second time. Ask if anyone in the class can explain the display and say where the hands on a clock face would be at that time.

After viewing

Recap
- Talk through the programme with the children. Encourage them to use their own words to describe what they have seen and heard. Ask questions like:
  - Why were Sam and Amber unsure how long they would have to wait when they were first trapped in the junk chute?
  - How did Numberella explain the use of am and pm?
  - What happened after Numberella had gone?
  - What did Sam and Amber do to pass the time?
  - How did they manage to free themselves?
- Have a whole-class oral session where the children have opportunities to give times using analogue and digital clocks. Construct a grid, as in the diagram, with some spaces. Ask individual children to come and complete different parts.

Time: in words	Time: analogue	Time: 12 hour digital
Three o'clock in the afternoon.	3:00pm	03:00

Time words
- Discuss the number of words we have that are connected with telling the time and the passing of time. Ask the children to write a time spiral of words starting from the centre of an A4 piece of paper. How many words do they know? See Activity Sheet 38.1 in the Star Maths 4 Activity Book for a time word search.

What happens during a day?
- Have a collection of different clocks and watches on display. Ask the children to keep a record, hour by hour, of their activities for a day starting at midnight and ending the following midnight. Ask the children to transfer their information to a pie chart if appropriate. Have a discussion about the information collected.

Cross-curricular links
- Science experiments provide good opportunities for children to gain experience of reading times accurately on digital and analogue clocks, as well as some idea of the passing of time. Set up an experiment such as 'What can you do in one minute?' Arrange for the children to work in pairs. They then take turns to time each other doing various tasks such as calculations, writing out words they find difficult to spell and so on.
- A variation is for them to do nothing for a minute. One partner has the timer. The other has to say 'now' when they think a minute has passed. Partners should have at least three tries. Does accuracy improve with experience?

Reading timetables
- Have a selection of local bus and train timetables. Use them to construct a simple table on the board or flipchart that you can use to pose questions to the class. Using local names makes the reading of timetables easier and more interesting for the children.

Time problems
- Have a session talking about different time problems and how to solve them. Include problems like:

> The football match started at 2:30pm. The teams played 45 minutes each way and there was a break of 10 minutes at half time. At what time did the game end?
>
> A train leaves the station at 13:00 for a journey to the nearest city lasting three-quarters of an hour. At what time should it arrive?

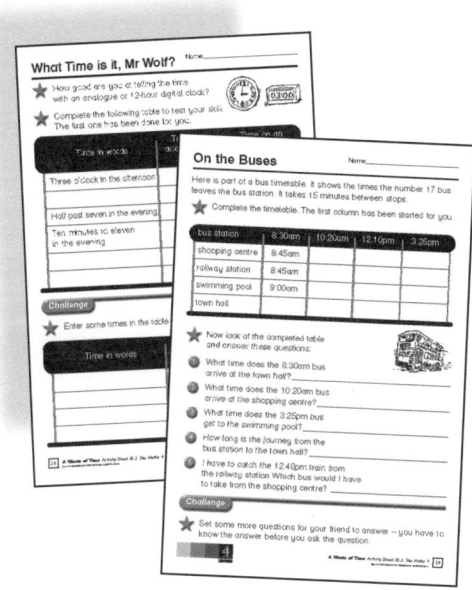

STAR MATHS
PROGRAMME 39

The Farewell Party

Programme outline

Botler is in charge of the music at Sam and Amber's leaving party. He is making sure the children have a great time. Uncle Zak has arranged a surprise game that involves watching clips of film taken during their visit and searching for hidden numbers. They have to write the numbers on cards. The four numbers they find are 2, 5, 9 and 14.

To unlock their surprise, Sam and Amber have to say the next number in the sequence. They try one or two ideas but have to call Numberella to help them. Numberella explains that the differences between the numbers are increasing so the next number in the sequence is 20.

Sam and Amber enter number 20 into the snakeliser and this activates a zimmerjet holding a model of the compound – a splendid surprise leaving present from Uncle Zak.

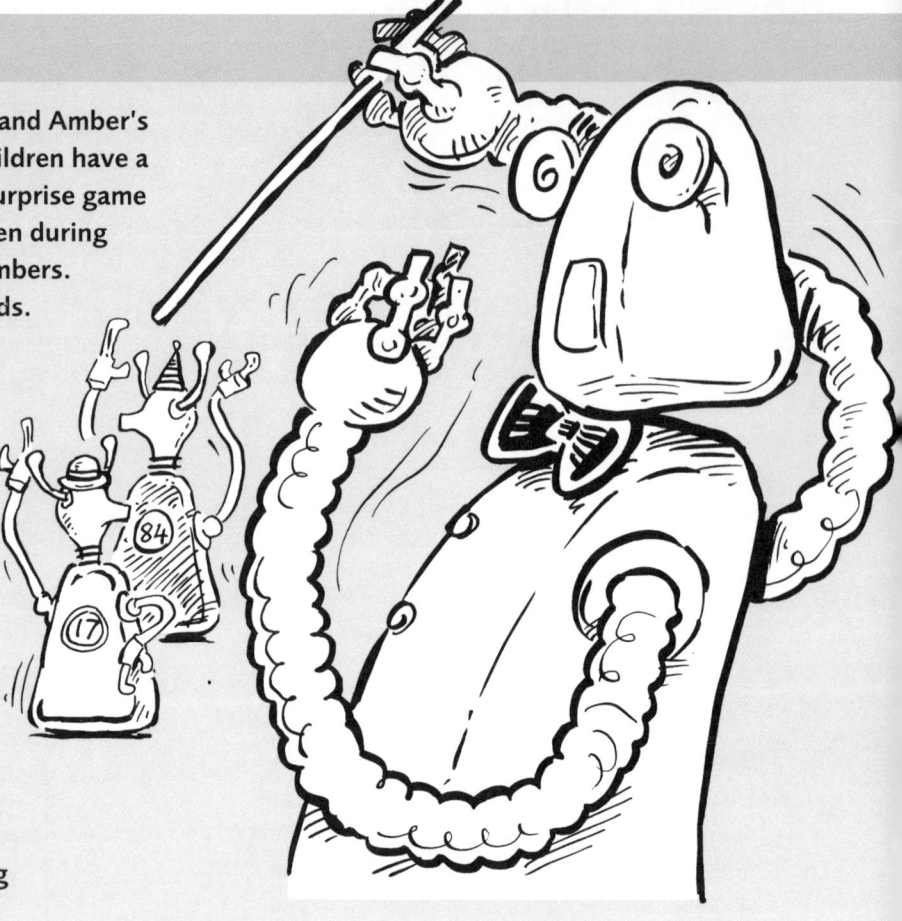

Learning outcomes

Children should gain experience of:

- solving mathematical problems and puzzles

Vocabulary

answer
calculate
how did you work it out?
method
operation
predict

right
sign
symbol
what could we try next?
wrong

Before viewing

☐ Talk about previous puzzles the children may have come across. Have one or two simple problems for the children to tackle like:

- What would be the next three numbers in these sequences: 17, 15, 13?   4, 8, 12, 16?

☐ Allow the children to talk to their neighbour about the problems and ways of finding the answers.

While viewing

☐ Pause the tape, if you wish, when Sam and Amber are trying to work out the next number in the sequence. Sam thinks it might be something to do with the differences between the numbers and he calls Numberella. Ask if anyone in the class can suggest what the next number in the sequence might be and explain their reasoning.

After viewing

Recap

☐ Spend some time going over the programme. Encourage the children to share what they have seen and heard. Ask questions like:

- Why was Botler playing music pattern number 364?
- What was the surprise game that Uncle Zak introduced?
- What were the numbers Amber and Sam discovered?
- What was the next challenge in the game?
- Why did Sam and Amber call Numberella?
- What did Numberella demonstrate?

Number sequence challenges

☐ Have a whole-class session talking about number sequences. Give the class several sequences to work on. Then, after discussing the next few numbers of the sequences, put the class into two teams to think of new sequences and challenge the other team to find the next three numbers. Encourage the children to start with sequences using their multiplication tables.

100-square challenges

☐ Play the game 'What number's in my pocket?' Display a large 1–100 square. Tell the children you are thinking of a number between 1 and 100 and you want them to guess what it is. They can ask you questions about the number but you can only answer 'yes' or 'no'. You want them to try to guess the number in as few questions as possible. After several tries have a class discussion about sensible strategies and the sort of questions to ask, such as: is it more than 50? Or, is it an odd number?

Find the secret number

☐ Tell the children you want them to write some numbers in code for their friends to discover. The code is based on the 1–100 square and you generate new numbers using arrows. For example, consider the code 52 ↑↑↑ → →. What secret number does this code generate? Tell the children to look at the number 52 on the 100-square. Then use the arrows to find the secret number.

☐ After spending a little time exploring secret numbers with the whole class, let the children work in pairs, giving each other secret numbers to find.

Find the missing digits

☐ Calculation exercises can be turned into challenges by giving children the answer and asking them to find the missing numbers or digits. For example:

3? + ?8 = 130

5? − ?9 = 28

Have a whole-class discussion about methods to use. Talk about inverse operations and encourage the children to share their ways of working with the rest of the class. How do they know which digit to use? How can they check they are right?

Real-life problems

☐ Write five or six problems on the board or flipchart. Tell the children you want them to work with a partner to decide which operation is needed to work out the answer to the problem. Then ask the children to complete the problems. Having given the children time to complete the problems, discuss them with the whole class. Do not merely give answers. Get the children to explain what they understood by the problem, what method they used to solve it and whether they checked to make sure they were right by using an inverse operation.

Some children have difficulty with one or more of the stages of problem solving:

- Understanding the problem
- Knowing what operation to use
- Doing the calculation accurately
- Relating the answer to the original question to make sure it makes sense

Discussion of all these aspects of problem solving will be valuable for most children.

More activities

☐ See the Star Maths 4 Activity Book for other games and activities.

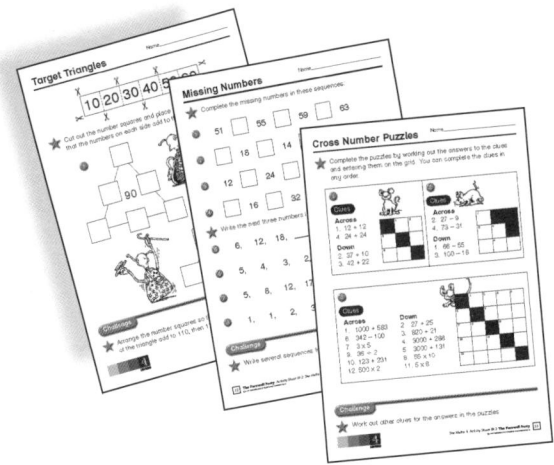

52 ↑↑↑ → → = 24

STAR MATHS
PROGRAMME 40
The Final Mission

Programme outline

Sam and Amber are waiting for Lisa to arrive to take them home when Uncle Zak has his attention drawn to the co-ordinate screen by the Pozzle. He sees that the tiny Wattbot is lost – he seems to have misread the given co-ordinates. Uncle Zak sets off to rescue him, much to Amber's relief, although Botler worries that he will not be back in time to say goodbye to Sam and Amber.

As Uncle Zak sets out, the children see a large shadow following him. They want to send a rescue Wattbot but don't know how to give the correct co-ordinates. They call Numberella who explains how to read and write co-ordinates.

Amber and Sam work out a safe route and Uncle Zak arrives back at the very last minute before they take off. He has with him a Krizwok to show the children. It is a really tiny creature that throws a large shadow as a defence mechanism. Uncle Zak says Sam can take it home if he likes, then he reaches in his pocket for a present for Amber – the tiny Wattbot.

Learning outcomes

Children should gain experience of:

- solving problems using co-ordinates

Vocabulary

along	direction	row
axes	explain your method	select
axis	grid	solve
calculate	horizontal	through
column	journey	towards
co-ordinates	origin	vertical
diagonal	position	work out

While viewing

- Pause the tape, if you wish, when Numberella says to Amber and Sam 'you can't go straight to (3, 4)'. Ask if anyone in the class can suggest a safe route for the rescue Wattbot to take.

Before viewing

- Spend some time with the class revising previous work on describing positions and movement. Use a floor robot, if possible, to demonstrate the effect of giving a sequence of instructions. Or have one of the children acting as a robot receiving instructions from the rest of the class.

After viewing

Recap

☐ Spend some time going over the programme. Encourage the children to put what they have seen and heard into their own words. Prompt them by asking questions like:

- Why did Uncle Zak dash off in the zimmerjet just before Sam and Amber were due to leave?
- Why did Sam and Amber decide to send a rescue Wattbot after Uncle Zak?
- Why did they have to call Numberella?
- What did Numberella explain?
- How did they find a safe route for the Wattbot to take?
- What extra presents did the children take home with them?
- What is the point (0, 0) called?

☐ Talk about the importance of giving co-ordinates in the right order. It is a convention that the horizontal co-ordinate is given before the vertical co-ordinate. Remind the class of the mountain rescue services who find their work so much easier if they have an accurate grid reference. See if they can come up with a saying that helps them remember the right order for giving co-ordinates.

Treasure island

☐ Draw a simple 'treasure island' map on the board, using a 5 x 5 or 6 x 6 grid. Mark several relevant details on the grid such as hills, caves, swamps and the treasure. Point out the horizontal and the vertical axes and ask the children to read the position of various features. Write the co-ordinates of the different places on the board. Then, when the children are fairly confident with this activity, explain that you want them to be able to find certain places on the treasure map using co-ordinates you will give them.

Vocabulary poster

☐ Make a large poster of the vocabulary associated with describing position and direction. Display it in a prominent position in the classroom. After talking about the words and their spellings on several occasions, take down the poster and have a spelling competition. Ask for volunteers for a spelling bee or have a 'Master Mind' competition.

'Master Mind' competition

☐ Position a suitable chair at the front of the classroom and ask for volunteers. Competitors could be asked for the spellings and meanings of several words, or to think of a sentence using several words to illustrate their meanings.

Story challenge

☐ This is another activity using some of the words on the vocabulary poster. Arrange the class in groups of about four or five, and give each group a selection of the words, together with other words of ordinary everyday objects. They have to make up a story to include all their words. Allow time for groups to think about their story and write it out. Then have a session where the groups read out their story to the rest of the class.

'Initial' co-ordinates

☐ Give the children squared paper and ask them to draw their initials, using upper-case letters. They must use straight lines only so there will need to be some discussion as to how to represent letters such as O or D. Children make a note of the co-ordinates and exchange them with a friend who tries to draw the initials from the co-ordinates given.

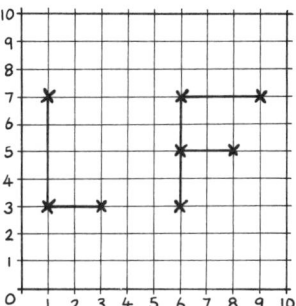

☐ Extend this activity by letting the children draw a simple picture on squared paper and then convert it into a set of co-ordinates. Then let friends try and draw the picture from the set of co-ordinates. Alternatively use Resource Sheet 3, Co-ordinate Pictures, on page 28.

More activities

☐ See the Star Maths 4 Activity Book for other games and activities.

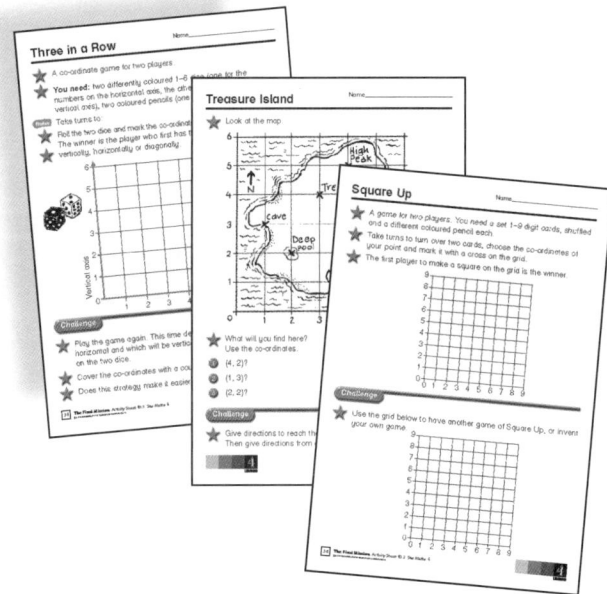

Palindromes and the Seven Times Table

 A number is a palindrome that stays the same when its digits are written in reverse order.

For example: | 33 | | 252 | | 767 | | 123 321 |

 Some numbers are palindromes and are also divisible by seven.

For example: | 77 | | 161 |

1. Use your calculator to make a list of numbers divisible by seven.

2. What are the palindromes between 100 and 199 that are divisible by seven?

3. Investigate these numbers. Can you spot a pattern or rule?

4. Write down all the palindromes between 1000 and 9999 that are divisible by seven.

   Can you still use your previous rule?

STAR MATHS 4
RESOURCE SHEET 2

Time Loop Cards

7:25am 1 hour later	**9:00am** 20 minutes earlier	**7:45am** 1 hour and 20 minutes later	**4:30pm** 10 minutes later
8:25am 5 minutes earlier	**8:40am** 1 hour later	**9:05am** 1 hour and 25 minutes later	**20 minutes to 5 in the afternoon** 30 minutes later
8:20am 10 minutes later	**9:40am** 5 minutes earlier	**10:30am** 90 minutes later	**5:10pm** 25 minutes earlier
8:30am 15 minutes later	**9:35am** 2 hours earlier	**12 noon** 5 hours later	**a quarter to 5 in the afternoon** 1 hour and 20 minutes later
a quarter to 9 in the morning quarter of an hour later	**7:35am** 10 minutes later	**5:00pm** 30 minutes earlier	**6:05pm** 13 hours and 20 minutes later

© 2001 CHANNEL FOUR TELEVISION CORPORATION

Co-ordinate Pictures

Here are some pictures on grids.
Write down the co-ordinates of the crosses in order.
Always start at the cross marked 'START'.

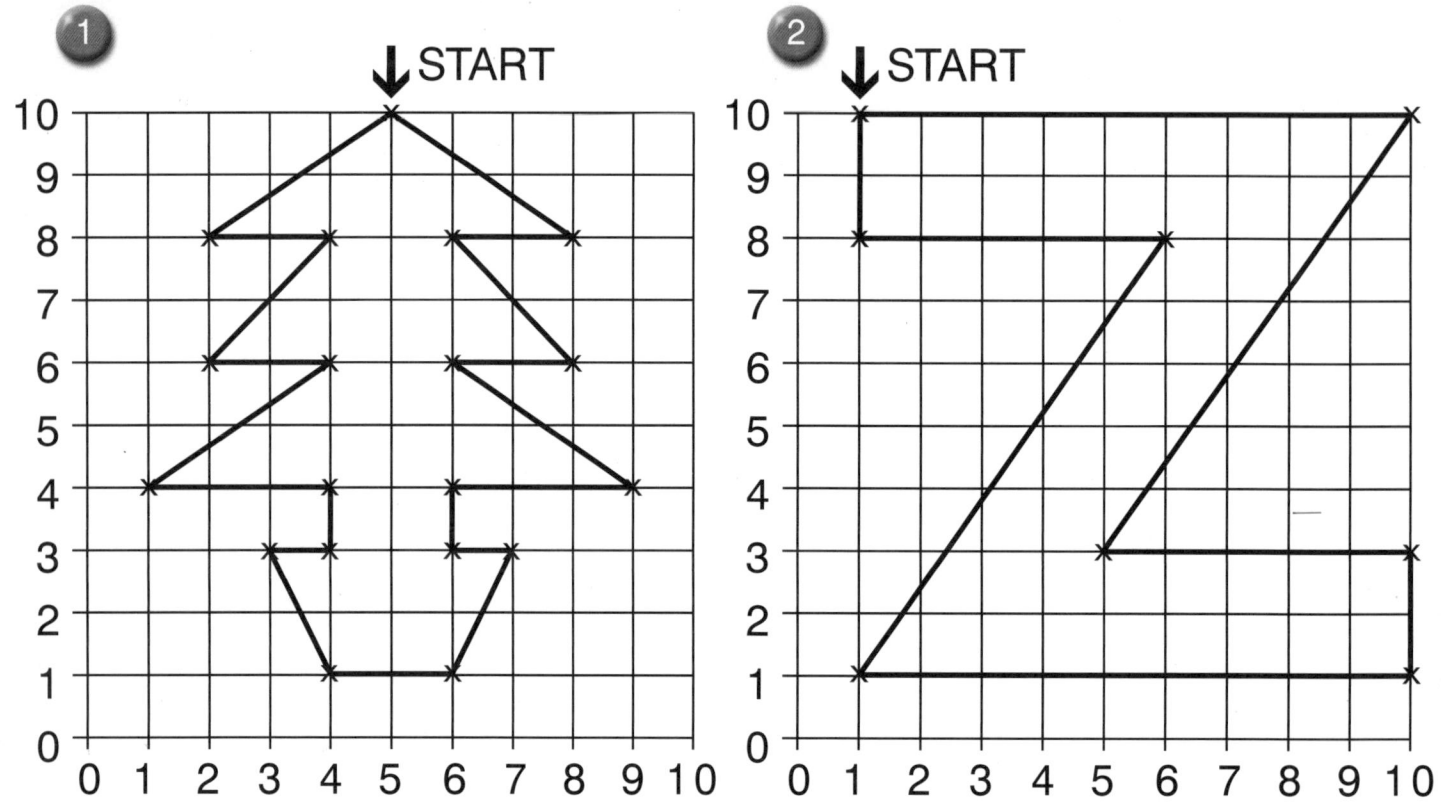

3) Draw a grid on squared paper, mark it up to ten across and up.

Plot these points and join them up in order:
(1, 1) (1, 7) (3, 7) (3, 3) (7, 3) (7, 1) (1, 1)

What 'picture' have you made?